Figure 1. *Ishi* .
(Courtesy of Lowie Museum of Anthropology, University of California at Berkeley.)

Author Richard Burrill at Deer Creek.

On the Cover: Neg. Trans. No. 317047 (photo circa 1913 of Ishi by Joseph Dixon of the Rodney Wanamaker Expedition of Citizenship). Courtesy Department Library Services American Museum of Natural History. With special thanks to Barbara Mathe of Photographic Collection.

Cover design by Grant Gibbs with motif by artist David Ipiña, Yurok, artist.

Printed in the U.S.A.

THE ANTHRO COMPANY
P.O. Box 661765
Sacramento, CA 95866-1765
U.S.A.

Library of Congress Cataloging in Publication Data.

Burrill, Richard
Ishi: America's Last Stoneage Indian

1. Yana Indians
2. Indians of North America
3. California Indians

ISBN 1-878464-01-9 (pbk.) ISBN 1-878464-00-0 (cloth)

ISHI:

America's Last Stone Age Indian

By Richard Burrill

Richard Burrill
March 9, 1994

The Anthro Company

P. O. Box 661765
Sacramento, CA 95866-1765

THE ANTHRO COMPANY

THE ANTHRO COMPANY is a small company of artists and educators with headquarters in Sacramento, California. We are working for a better world. Through the discipline of anthropology, we address humankind's relationship with the natural world as well as the issue of inequality between peoples and genders worldwide. We recognize that human survival is contingent upon the continued existence of a diversity of human communities, and will guide our activities accordingly. To our students, we owe nondiscriminatory access to our seminars, and shall provide training which is informed, accurate, and relevant to the needs of the larger society. We serve both professional anthropologists and their students, as well as intelligent lay people who simply like anthropology in and of itself.

Items Distributed

Sold are anthropology books, essay reprints, flat prints, maps, posters, and art pieces by select artists. Anthropology film classics and tapes will also be sold as permissions are being secured. An *Events and Travel Bulletin Board* is another service to be provided by THE ANTHRO COMPANY.

Dedication

Dedicated, with respectful admiration, to two great people: J. Martin (Mike) Weber and Thomas Waterman. Mr. Weber has done as much as any one person to protect the natural habitat of greater Sacramento. He has been a science teacher and environmental educator for Portland High School in Oregon and then the Sacramento County Office of Education since 1949. He was instrumental in the publication of *The Outdoor World of the Sacramento Region: Field Guide Edition* (1975), helped establish the Effie Yeaw Interpretive Center, and produced *Chen-Kut-Pam*, the movie about Marie Potts, the Maidu Indian educator. Mike Weber also felt this story, now in book form, was "the finest essay he had ever read about Ishi."

Thomas T. Waterman, anthropology professor at the University of California, Berkeley, went to Oroville, sat down with the weary Ishi, and said the magic word *siwini*, which Ishi recognized. Waterman also carefully investigated and artfully described Grizzly Bear's Hiding Place afterwards so this story could be more fully told.

Figure 2. ***Ishi*** **by** ***artist Carol Mathis of Friday House Gallery in Placerville, CA.*** **(Reprinted courtesy of Herb Puffer.)**

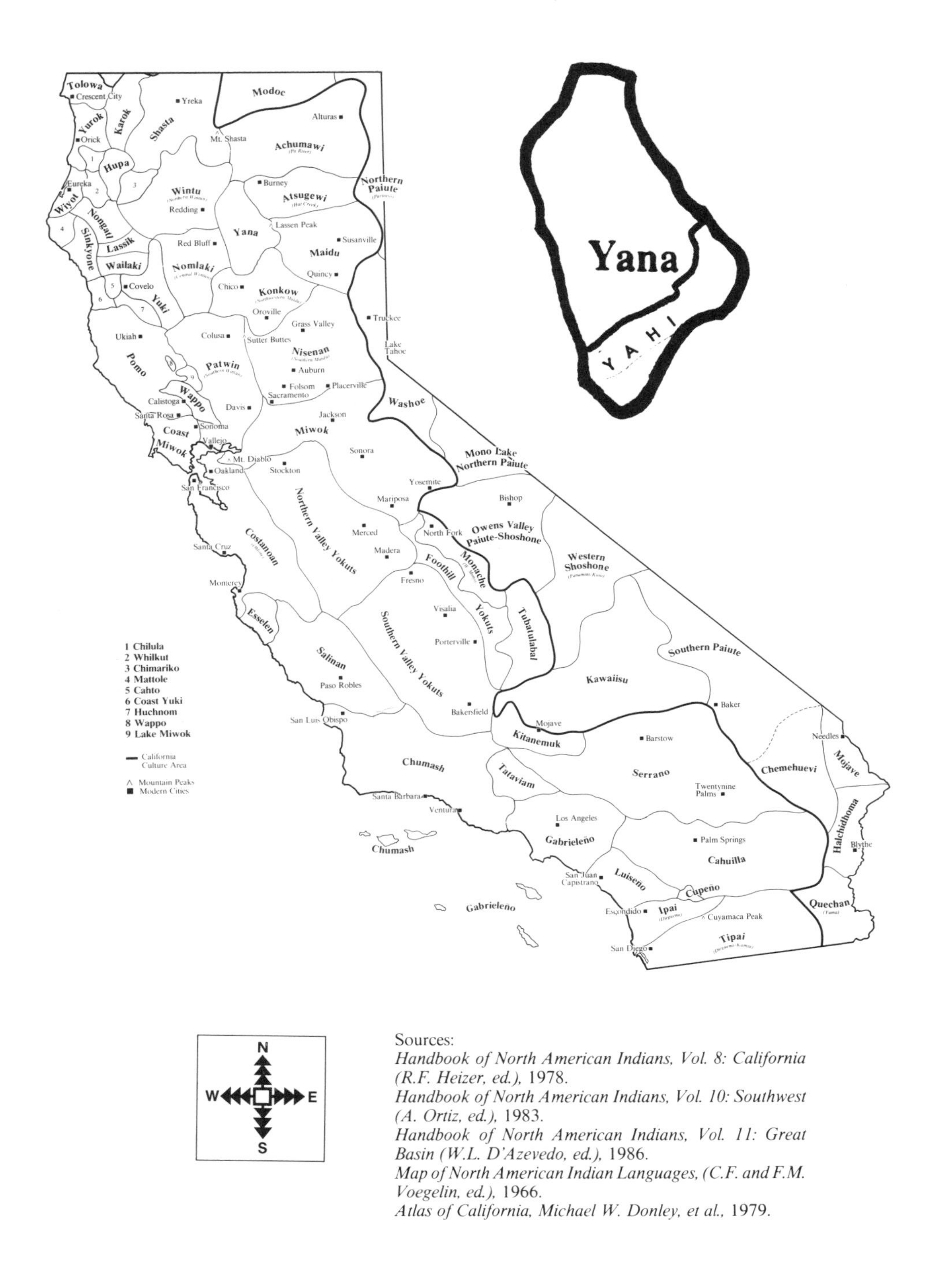

Sources:
Handbook of North American Indians, Vol. 8: California (R.F. Heizer, ed.), 1978.
Handbook of North American Indians, Vol. 10: Southwest (A. Ortiz, ed.), 1983.
Handbook of North American Indians, Vol. 11: Great Basin (W.L. D'Azevedo, ed.), 1986.
Map of North American Indian Languages, (C.F. and F.M. Voegelin, ed.), 1966.
Atlas of California, Michael W. Donley, et al., 1979.

Figure 3. Map: *Tribal Map of California*
Ishi's home territory
(Courtesy of Herb Putter)

America's Last Stoneage Indian

By Richard Burrill

The story of Ishi is one of the most remarkable in the annals of Indians on this continent. The discovery of the "wild" Indian camp in 1908, where Ishi had lived, without firearms, hidden from white men for more than forty years, and his emergence at Oroville, California in 1911, is, without exaggeration, one of the great American stories.

The story of Ishi, the last of his Yahi tribe, begins just outside the town of Oroville on the evening of August 29, 1911, in the corral of a slaughterhouse. In justice to Ishi, his own version of his "capture" should be given:

> *His people were all dead, he said. A woman and a child had been drowned in crossing a stream. The old woman found by the surveyors [1908] was dead. For some time [about three years] he had been entirely alone — poor, often hungry, with nothing to live for. This, by the way, was no doubt the reason for his drifting, perhaps aimlessly, so far southward of his old home. One day he made up his mind to "come in." He expected to be killed, he said, but that no longer mattered. So he walked westward all day, without meeting anyone, and at dusk came to a house where meat was hung up. Tired, hungry, and thirsty, he sat down. Soon a boy came out with a lantern, saw him, recoiled, and called a man, who ran up.*[1]

The boy's name was Floyd Phillip Heffner, and the man was Adolf F. Kessler, who was responsible for Ishi's "capture." Mr. Kessler was the first white man ever to lay a hand on him. He personally revealed on tape his experience in detail, intended to clear up some misleading views presented by other writers concerning the time of day and the circumstances involved.[2]

Floyd Heffner, a lad of ten years, lived close by. He frequently helped the butchers with odd jobs. He was asked to get the horses from the slaughterhouse corral. With halter in hand, he climbed atop the fence when the unusually restless horses caused him to scan the V-shaped corral area. He noticed a man, motionless, on his haunches, with his back against the barn. Excited, the boy yelled to the butchers behind him, "There's a man up here!"

Kessler answered, "I'm coming right up!" Responding to Floyd's excited voice, Kessler grabbed a gambrel* with which to protect himself and hurried to the spot of discovery.[3]

Could this be one of those Mexicans earlier accused of stealing meat? Were they back for more? Kessler recalled:

> *Being short of breath from running and a little over-anxious, I jerked him out from his squatting position and threw questions at him pretty fast, but got no response whatever. I felt provoked by his reticence, so I grabbed him by the shoulder forcing him to the ground, and he just lay on his side. In no manner did he resist the rough treatment, so I let go of him.*[4]

They called Sheriff John B. Webber from Oroville by telephone who reluctantly came out, barely believing their story of the "wild man". In the dim light cast by an oil lantern, the sheriff viewed Ishi, who was broken, emaciated from starvation and surely the object of pity. He noticed that Ishi's hair was recently singed and his

* a tool used to hang carcasses

body was coated with black pitch [later recognized as Indian rites for mourning]. The man wore an old undershirt worn off to his midriff and a black mandarin Chinese jacket, much like a pajama top (see Figure 4). He was barefoot. Sheriff Webber looked closely at Ishi's face and noted his earlobes through which a buckskin string had been drawn. His nose held a small, wooden nose plug [awarded by his tribe at puberty, and to be worn at death to help guarantee passage to the other world]. The sheriff placed handcuffs upon Ishi, called for a butcher's coat apron to cover him, and placed him in a wagon to carry him toward the bright lights of the city. In this condition, Ishi stood for his first photograph (see Figure 4).

Ishi recalled being taken to a "large and fine house" - the jail - and very kindly treated and well fed by a "big chief" - the deputy sheriff. From there the news spread.

Reading the newspapers in San Francisco were Alfred Kroeber, Professor of anthropology at the University of California and professor Thomas T. Waterman, also an anthropologist. They both guessed at once that this represented a unique case. If the strange man actually spoke an unknown language, could he not be one of the last survivors of a supposedly vanished tribe? Quickly exchanging telegrams to Oroville, Professor Waterman journeyed by train to the jail, armed with a brief list of Northern and Central Yana words. (The languages of the two northern tribes of this geographical area had been somewhat preserved, but not a word of the language of the Southern Yana tribe, the Yahi, had ever been recorded. The Yahi tribe was considered extinct.)

Theodora Kroeber described what happened when Waterman finally arrived in Oroville and sat down beside Ishi with his phonetically transcribed list of Yana words:

Figure 4. *Ishi, August 29, 1911.*
(Courtesy of Lowie Museum of Anthropology,
University of California at Berkeley.)

[Waterman] began to read from it, repeating each word, pronouncing it as well as he knew how, Ishi was attentive but unresponding until, discouragingly far down the list, Waterman said siwini which means yellow pine, at the same time tapping the pine framework of the cot on which they sat. Recognition lit up the Indian's face. Waterman said the magic word again; Ishi repeated it after him, correcting his pronunciation, and for the next moments the two of them banged at the wood of the cot, telling each other over and over, siwini, siwini.[5]

At last, the difficult first sound recognition was achieved! Ishi and Waterman tried out more and more words and phrases. They finally began to communicate. Ishi was indeed one of the lost tribe. He was a Yahi!

Professor Waterman made arrangements for the Indian to live in San Francisco at the University, within the confines of the Museum of Anthropology. It was here he received the name by which we know him.

Until this time, Ishi was referred to as the "wild man" or the "mysterious Indian." Sam Batwi, a still surviving Northern Yana interpreter who spoke a somewhat related dialect, asked him his name (see Figure 5). To all inquiries, Ishi shook his head saying that he had been alone so long that he had no one to name him. (This was really a polite fiction. The etiquette of Ishi's part of the world demanded that a person never tell his own name, at least, not in reply to a direct request.) Professor Kroeber decided to call him "Ishi," because it was the Yana word for "man." Ishi accepted his name fully, and even to his death never told anyone his real name.

To understand how this truly aboriginal man and a handful of his tribe could have escaped "civilization"

Figure 5. *Sam Batwi, Alfred Kroeber, Ishi, 1911.*
(Courtesy of Lowie Museum of Anthropology,
University of California at Berkeley.)

until 1911, we must turn back the clock. We must visualize the world from which Ishi came and why his case was such good fortune for science. For Ishi's life had followed the curve of a tragedy of classical Greek proportions; the tragedy of an entire people's downfall.

A little more than a hundred years ago, there lived three to four hundred Yahi Indians along Mill Creek and Deer Creek. Here in the southern Cascade foothills west of snow-capped Mount Lassen, called *wa ganu p'a,* was the first world of Ishi. He and his people lived by hunting and fishing. They looked to *wa ganu p'a,* the great volcano with its mystical face and potentially eruptive spirits, as a resting place of The Creator. It was a divine place from which to gain balance and power. The Yahi believed in powerful magic and powerful visions as well as good and evil spirits.

In the summertime, the Yahi would camp along the upper regions of this magical mountain and hunt deer in the cooler summer breezes. During the winter, the Yahi would migrate to the lower elevations along Mill Creek and Deer Creek. There, during the season of the falling acorn (September), the Indians would gather acorns among the black and valley oak groves to make mush and bread. Then, too, salmon filled the Yahi streams, another wonderful food source.

The Yahi, using spears and nets, knew never to fish too far downstream away from Mount Lassen's protection. Yahi legend forewarned their children of "fabulous malignant water grizzlies" called *ha t'an en* that lived in the waters along the Sacramento River, who would pull fishermen down to devour them.[6] For these reasons, the Yahi became referred to as the independent and provincial plateau Indians or "Mill Creek Indians." Indeed, it was largely this dense and wild hill country, their expert familiarity with it, and their protective pride towards it

Figure 6. ***Manzanita above Deer Creek.***
(Reprinted courtesy of Robert L. Burrill.)

that helped them survive undaunted for so long.

Summer followed winter and winter followed summer in a never ending progression. Life continued as it always had. But suddenly time had meaning. Gold was discovered at Sutter's Mill! Gold was in the foothills! Miners poured across the crest of the Peter Lassen Trail between Mill Creek and Deer Creek — through the heart of the Yahi country.

Prospectors and vigilantes drove the Indians off of the salmon creeks. They destroyed the native food sources through hydraulic mining. Herds of cattle trampled the vegetation in the canyons.

The Yahi were forced to raid the encroaching white rangers' cabins. While the Yahi resisted, the fight was unequal and violence only escalated. After years of guerrilla warfare, the Yahi were practically exterminated by the white man.

The last massacre, the Kingsley Cave episode in 1865, involved the slaughter of thirty Yahi, including young children and babies. A party of four vaqueros, using dogs, pursued a band of Indians to avenge the killing of one steer, found shot with an arrow and partly butchered. They located some Indians in a cave on Mill Creek. Shooting a number of them, they finally entered the cave itself. Here they found some dried meat, and some small children. The four armed men forthwith killed them all. Norman Kingsley, one of the killers, later described himself as "being a humane man, a person of fine sensibilities and delicacy of feeling."[7] He explained about the murders that he had exchanged his:

> *. . . 56-caliber Spencer rifle for a .38-caliber Smith and Wesson revolver, because the rifle "tore them up so bad," particularly the babies.*[8]

Figure 7. ***Deer Creek Country, north side.***
(Reprinted courtesy of Robert L. Burrill.)

Five survivors took refuge in the wild canyon of Deer Creek, and the last recorded time that anyone saw them was in 1870. There were two men, two women, and a child. This was Ishi, for he later told how, "when he was a small boy, 'so high,' the white men came at sunrise and killed his people in their camp."[9]

By 1872, it was quiet in the hills. The Yahi were thought to have been entirely exterminated by starvation or exposure. Nevertheless, a remnant of the tribe concealed themselves in the canyon territory three miles long and half-a-mile wide. They held out against civilization for forty years from 1870 until 1910. This devoted band remained completely hidden away, preserving an absolute independence. They were — without a doubt — the smallest group of free people in the world!

For weeks on end, they never left a footprint. When they traveled, they stepped from rock to rock, or followed the creek beds, or crawled through passages in the brush too small for even a deer to get through. They kept close watch on the trails, and never showed themselves, except for these few reports that most people in the Sacramento Valley simply ignored:

1894 - Elijah Graham, exasperated at the persistent robbing of his cabin, decided to punish the thief by leaving a sack of poisoned flour on his porch. To avoid accidents, he wrote a plain notice that the flour was poisoned and left it where it could be seen. The flour, nevertheless, promptly disappeared. This, Graham cited, was proof that there were Indians in the country who were robbing cabins. Hardly anyone took him seriously.

15 Years Later — Historical Site Vanishes

Figure 8. *Elijah Graham's Cabin Site in July 1972* (Photograph by Richard L. Burrill.)

Figure 9. *Elijah Graham's Cabin Site in July 1987* (Photograph by Richard L. Burrill.)

Both Figures 8 and 9 are testimony to how quickly historical sites literally vanish, save for a few foundational ground stones. Both posted trail signs and maps identify this clearing on the north side of Deer Creek as Graham's Pinery. Anyone who has read the Ishi story knows it was here in 1894, on this very porch, where cattle rancher Elijah Graham set out poison in retaliation for Indians robbing his cabin. Notice that in a span of just fifteen years, only one of the large house timbers remains barely visible in the right foreground. The timbers were most likely used for firewood by visiting campers.

Whether this episode reduced the number of the Yahi or not, we do not know (see Figures 8 & 9).[10]

1894 - Mr. D.B. Lyon and his brother found what they at first believed was a bear track near Mill Creek. It turned out to be a barefoot human track, very wide across the toes. The individual evidently had not worn shoes, for this foot is very calloused, with cracks across the bottom. They followed his tracks, but, evidently, the Indian found he was being pursued and he jumped from the top of a bluff into the top of a tree and escaped. Lyon remarked to his brother that he would not make the same descent for any sum (see Figures 8 & 9).

1906 - The cabin at the Occidental mine, operated by Mr. Gillenwater along with two employees, was robbed. Among other things, what is called in the country a "war bag" — in other words, a U.S. Army duffle bag, was taken.

1908 - W.D. Polk and K. Crowder were camped at the Speegle place, where Sulphur Creek joins Deer Creek. They went down Deer Creek a mile or so, and anticipating an Indian visit, one of them slipped back along under the edge of the bluff with a "30-30" rifle. The Indians, as a matter of fact, were just preparing to carry off the staples from the cabin. They took alarm, and dashed across Deer Creek. One of them in his haste dropped his headgear, which the whites picked up. Nothing was left in the cabin but a little rice and some canned stuff. An effort was made to track them, but they were too cunning. They stepped only on rocks where they left no footprints and took to the water so that they could not be followed with dogs.[11]

This brings the history of the Yahi to its final phase. On the evening of November 9, 1908, two young surveyors were returning upstream to their camp about sunset. They were involved on a survey for the Oro Water, Light and Power Company which was considering the erection of a dam just below Sulphur Creek. By the margin of the creek they suddenly saw a naked Indian standing on a rock, armed with a long spear (see Figure 10). The Indian was undoubtedly looking for his supper with a fish-spear, but his wild look startled both men. The two surveyors beat a quick path back to camp where their story was received with varying emotions.

The next morning, however, J. M. Apperson went downstream with another man to see what they could find. Mr. Apperson was convinced that Indian people still lived in this region. They went on the south side of the creek and began working through the thick brush on

Figure 10.
Ishi in 1914 standing on a rock, armed with a long spear.
(Courtesy of Lowie Museum of Anthropology, University of California at Berkeley.)

the steep hillside above the stream. An arrow was shot at him, which narrowly missed. After some debate, they turned back.

In the meantime, the surveying party went back to work, chopping out their flume line to convey impounded water down the canyon to a projected power plant below. By ten o'clock in the morning they had ascended about five hundred feet above the south side of the creek when they suddenly walked into an Indian encampment. Two Indians, running as if for their lives, were actually seen. One was an old man, who was helped along by a middle-aged woman. They escaped over a rock slide and vanished in the direction of the cliffs.

The surveyors and their companions advanced cautiously and explored the habitation. Baskets, blankets of skins, points of harpoons for spearing salmon, bows and arrows, and other native tools were scattered about, mixed with jute and flour bags, knives, saws, files, and tools, some of which were later identified by their owners as stolen from neighboring cabins.

Inside the camp and under some blankets, they also found a partially paralyzed old woman, trembling and frightened nearly to death and unable to move. The white men did what they could for this old person. Apperson gave her a drink out of a nearby canteen which had evidently been filled at the creek below. The whites then helped themselves to the contents of the camp, and then left. When they returned the next day, to satisfy their curiosity further, no Indians were about, and even the old woman was gone. Her people evidently came back and carried her away to some other unknown shelter.

Three structures were also found in camp, all of which were in the midst of a perfectly impenetrable jungle. One was a shelter of pepperwood boughs, with a frame work of rough poles. Just under cover of some large laurel trees, it was indistinguishable to any river travelers below (see Figure 11). A second shelter close by, heavily smoked and showing marks of very long occupation, was made of pieces of driftwood, old wagon canvas, and some odds and ends. There was a third A-framed structure consisting of poles, firmly lashed together with bark. Inside the structure was a series of crossed-stick shelves raised a few feet above the ground. It was evidently used for smoking salmon (See Figure 12). All of these lodges were of tiny proportions, but rather cunningly put together. They called the camp in their language *Wowunupo'mu tetna,* which means "Bear's Hiding Place," because there were bear dens in this wilderness of brush and boulders in times before the Indians.

This site has since been visited by a number of people, scientific and otherwise, including this writer. There is no doubt that the entire encampment had been purposefully

Figure 11. ***Interior, Showing Drying Rack.***
(Courtesy of Lowie Museum of Anthropology, University of California at Berkeley)

Figure 12. ***Remnant of House Frame at Wowunopo.*** **(Courtesy of Lowie Museum of Anthropology, University of California at Berkeley.)**

arranged by a group of people who were desperately anxious to hide themselves and quite skilled in their disguise tactics (see Figures 11, 12, 13, 21, 22, 23).

Thomas Waterman explained:

> *The houses were built where they were invisible from the cliffs on either side. The Indians passed down to the creek, which was very important to them on account of the fish in it, under the shelter of growths of laurel. Thus, they could move about and still remain hidden. Moreover, they avoided making visible trails, especially near the water. The little path that led down from the lodges under and through the chaparral, diverted in many places and disappeared as it approached the stream. In other words, they continually went down to the water by different ways, to avoid making one conspicuous pathway. In making the paths*

through the brush, they bent aside the necessary twigs. Cutting or breaking them would have made the path much more conspicuous. Altogether, the place and its selection showed considerable evidence of craft, and to the wandering hunter or rider on the mountains round about, the locality would have always looked like a genuine bear's hiding place, for all the evidence of human habitation to be seen.

Ishi was not seen. He probably discharged the arrow which almost wounded Apperson. He was undoubtedly present, and possibly waiting for another good shot, when the camp was actually invaded. Since the whites were armed with revolvers, Ishi probably kept just out of sight, which was, of course, the best military strategy.

It is sad to think that all the artifacts and materials at Grizzly Bear's Hiding Place, taken in mere curiosity, meant the difference between survival and destruction to the poor Indians (see Figure 14). It is certain that as a group they were never heard of afterwards, and all but Ishi lost their lives as a result of fatigue, hunger, and exposure resulting from having to leave their camp. Not one gift did the white men leave to prove friendly intentions.

It is now known that Ishi, the last of his tribe, hunted and foraged alone through the woods for another three years until he could no longer find anything to eat. Then, in complete despair, Ishi walked westward all day, away from Mount Lassen, and outside of his provincial home base. He then sat down in the "slaughterhouse" of the world of 1911.

The second world of Ishi began in the San Francisco of 1911. On September 4, Ishi arrived at the U.C. Museum of Anthropology. His status was not entirely clear. Was Ishi an immigrant? Who would pay for Ishi's support?

Figure 13.
Buckeye plants camouflage cave entrance in proximity of Grizzly Bear's Hiding Place along the southern canyon wall above Deer Creek.
(Photograph by Richard Burrill 1973.)

Figure 14. *Merle Apperson posed under fur cape blanket taken from Yahi camp, 1908.* (From Eva Marie Apperson's *We Knew Ishi*, page 23.) A second cape is owned by the Chester Rose family of Chico, California. Mr. Rose was there when they found Ishi in Oroville.

He would not be permitted American citizenship (this wasn't afforded Indians until 1924). Nor was he a ward of a recognized reservation. Professor Kroeber solved the problem by placing him on the payroll as assistant janitor of the museum. The work was light and, to Ishi, interesting.

Ishi's adjustment to his new world could be compared to that of other individuals placed in foreign and unknown parts of the world today. Learning to tie a four-in-hand cravat, for instance, required only a single demonstration, since Ishi's experience included tying and knotting cords of hemp and hide. But wearing shoes did seem awkward. He held out against shoes for several months. When boarding for the first train trip in Oroville, Adolf Kessler recalled how "Ishi was carrying his shoes in his hands."[12] When asked if he would not like a pair to wear when he went outside in San Francisco he responded:

> *I see the ground is stone here. Walking on that all the time, I would wear out shoes, but my feet will never wear out.*[13]

Golden Gate Park was only three blocks from the museum. Occasionally, the man from the woods went there alone. He followed the park's meandering paths barefoot, again becoming intimate with animals and birds.

Ishi found running water and flush toilets were not only good, they were very, very clever conveniences, as were electric lights, switches, and gas stoves. Next to glue, Ishi rated matches as civilization's most important invention.

When someone gave Ishi a watch, he wore it as an article of pride and beauty with chain and pendant, but never kept it set. Ishi could "tell time" by his own system.

By some sun sense plus his simplified reading of the museum and hospital clocks, he knew midday and any hour which was pointed out. He was punctual in all his appointments, such as public interview hours on designated days.

Ishi learned to speak American English as fast as any foreigner does today. He preferred being with people rather than being alone. At first, it was the great number of people that frightened him. He was used to seeing no more than fifty people at once, when living in his Indian world. Ishi found and accepted the warmth of friendship that met him at the museum. It was the anthropologists' interest in Ishi's culture that encouraged Ishi to want to understand theirs.

It was fortunate that we knew Ishi. He taught us, by living example, that the absence of grand technology within a culture does not mean apathy of thought. Wisdom comes to cultures through experience. For instance, without a science laboratory, Ishi's people knew of a workable antidote for rattlesnake bite: the binding of a toad or frog on the affected area. Our scientists now know of a similar powerful alkaloid from the toad *Bufo nigra* called bufogin. In addition, the Pasteur Institute admits to the antidotal properties of salamander skin as a curative value in the immunization of guinea pigs bitten by the rattlesnake.[14]

Successful living so close to the land requires a wise use of native plants, herbs, and wildlife, which Ishi demonstrated. A twig of baywood or juniper placed in the nose septum was a built-in inhalator against colds. A Yahi equivalent for a book of matches was twirling a piece of buckeye plant upon a willow or cedar wood hearth. Boiled salmon skin made the best of glues. Milkweed made the most reliable cord or string.

In the spring of 1914, Alfred Kroeber, Thomas Waterman,

Dr. Saxton Pope and his son, and Ishi decided to take a camping trip to Deer Creek and Mill Creek so that Ishi could show them where and how he and his tribe actually lived. At first Ishi was nervous about returning to his canyons and the painful memories of his childhood and adult life. At last, Ishi gave himself over to the adventure, sharing places and recollections about his life and culture. Ishi showed them his home which enabled them to make a photographic record of Ishi hunting, fishing, swimming, and making a fire against a backdrop of Yahi streams and hills (see Figures 26, 27, 28, 29).

Ishi demonstrated his mastery of hunting by constructing a bow and arrows, and shooting a deer on the second day (see Figures 30, 31, 32, 33, 34).

> *As a hunter, it was [Ishi's] business to be aware of the presence of an animal before that animal was alerted to him. Sight, hearing, smell, all his senses seemed to contribute to this initial advantage of spotting an unsuspecting quarry (prey).*
>
> *Perhaps it was a rabbit he had seen or smelled. If so, he would remain hidden, but make a kissing sound with two fingers pressed against his lips: the soft, plaintive cry of a rabbit in distress (see Figure 15). While the inevitable rabbits drew near in response to this call, it was well for the hidden hunter to be prepared for more exciting game. A wildcat, mountain lion, coyote, or bear might also respond to this apparent invitation to an easy kill. In Ishi's repertory were also the different quail calls, the gray squirrel's squeak, the honk of wild geese, and many other bird and animal voices. He sometimes shot small game and birds from very nearby - a rabbit at five yards - or from as far away as forty yards. He shot birds in flight and animals*

running, but he preferred the still shot at close range. Because he was careful at all times to stay downwind from his prey, and because the bow is a silent weapon, animals were not alarmed even by an arrow which narrowly missed them. He lured them to him through rousing either their curiosity or their concern by means of his imitations, making sitting targets of them.

Figure 15. ***Ishi calling rabbits by making a kissing sound, 1914.*** **(Courtesy of Lowie Museum of Anthropology, University of California at Berkeley.)**

. . .Ishi preferred the tactic of lure and ambush to that of stalking or the chase. Crouched behind an artificially made cairn of rocks or behind or within a clump of bush close to where he had smelled or sighted or suspected the presence of deer, he would wait. He might imitate the whimper of a fawn by sucking on a madrone leaf folded between his lips. This was sure to bring out one or several does, uneasy for the safety of their young. Or he might put over his own head a stuffed deer's head, usually with antlers attached. Showing only the head over the top of rocks or bush, he would move about, cock it, simulate the nibbling of a leaf, and toss it. This device would bring a full-grown doe or buck deer within a few yards of him ... They might let an arrow or two whizz past; Ishi could expect to have opportunity to get the range and make a perfect hit before the deer, one or several, took alarm.[15]

Although the trip to Mill Creek and Deer Creek proved a big success, Ishi kept begging them to go home, and "home" to Ishi had become his room in the museum. Ishi stated he would "grow old in this house, and it is here I will die."[16]

After six adventurous and educational weeks, the expedition prepared to head back.[17] The members of the party discussed plans to repeat their trip in the fall. On May 30, 1914, shortly before the day that they would depart the old mountain, *Wa ganu pa'a* blew up! Smoke, steam, ashes, small rocks, and even boulders were hurled high into the air.[18] Was Mount Lassen expressing its displeasure? "If Ishi could only see that!" cried Eva Apperson as she pointed before the crowd in the street of Red Bluff.[19]

Figures 16 & 17. *On May 30, 1914, Mount Lassen erupted. This photograph of the eruption was taken June 14, 1914, as cited in B. F. Loomis' Pictorial History of the Lassen Volcano .* **(Mineral , California: Loomis Museum Association.) (Figure 17 Courtesy of artist Pat Darling, 1982.)**

Eva Marie Apperson, author of *We Knew Ishi*, wrote: *In the dense black smoke the likeness of a Bear's head was visible to the naked eye, then emerged gently in the image of a full-sized Bear shown sitting on its tail. Other scenes were visibly portrayed as the volume of smoke and ashes arose higher and was witnessed by hundreds of people on the streets of Red Bluff who were participating in a most memorable celebration, the first Macadamized paving of the two main streets in Red Bluff, May 30, 1914 and jointly with Memorial Day.* **(Courtesy of Suzanne Apperson.)**

Figures 18 and 19. *Two Faces in the Sky.*

Photographed on August 19, 1914 by one of the forest rangers and sent to R. E. Stinson for development, who, in turn, had the photo copyrighted. B. F. Loomis pp. 35-36 (Courtesy of B. F. Loomis.) Artist's sketch for Figure 19 unknown.

Mrs. Apperson stated, *This was not an imaginary thing, but manifestly practical and true to form as proof was in the seeing. From out of the dense mushroomed exhibit of smoke and ashes many signs and wonders were revealed... so realistic they were... a group of giants observed in a sitting position; special interest is of the two faces portrayed in the picturesque phenomena which gave the writer (Eva Apperson) an extra thrill, for it was shortly before this day that Ishi had departed the Mt. Lassen area on his last visit there—which was the height of his homeland, after a six week sojourn in Mill Creek and Deer Creek.* (Courtesy of Suzanne Apperson.)

From out of the dense mushroom of smoke and ash, appeared many signs and wonders. In the rising black smoke appeared the head of a great bear as if the bear was slowly emerging from out of the mountain's top (see Figures 16 & 17).[20] Was it *ha t'an en,* one of the fabulous malignant water grizzlies? Was it the power of the Creator?

Then emerged the upturned faces of two grand old men with an abundance of frosty white hair (see Fig. 18). Were these formidable Indian Grandfathers? There are no existing diaries or letters that mention Ishi's acknowledgment of this event.

In 1915, Ishi fell sick. On March 25, 1916, the last "wild" Indian of North America died of tuberculosis. He was unique, the last man of his world, and his change-over from the Stone Age to the post Iron Age was also unique. On Ishi's death, as his dearest Anglo friend, Dr. Saxton Pope wrote:

> *And so, stoic and unafraid, departed the last wild Indian of America. He closes a chapter in history. He looked upon us as sophisticated children — smart, but not wise. We knew many things, and much that is false. He knew nature, which is always true. His were the qualities of character that last forever. He was kind; he had courage and self-restraint, and though all had been taken from him, there was no bitterness in his heart. His soul was that of a child, his mind that of a philosopher.*[21]

Figure 20. *Ishi*
(Courtesy of Lowie Museum of Anthropology,
University of California at Berkeley.)

Figures 21 and 22.

Ishi's rock overhangs the immediate area of Sulfur Creek. In Ishi's day, the rock was used as an observation point. From it all trails leading in or out, or any activities round about from a higher level, could be observed. While in camp, 1914, Ishi was pleased to learn that the rock had been renamed for him. Merle Apperson is sitting on the rock.

(Taken from Eva Marie Apperson, *We Knew Ishi* (Red Bluff: Walker Lithograph Co., 1971, p.14).)

Figure 23. *Ishi's Rock on North Side of Deer Creek in the approximate vicinity of Bear's Hiding Place.* Photograph by Richard L. Burrill, 1987.)

Figure 24. *Ishi, May of 1914.*
(Courtesy of Lowie Museum of Anthropology, University of California at Berkeley.)

Figure 25. *Graham's Pinery on North Side of Deer Creek.*
(Photograph by Richard L. Burrill)

Changing hand positions

Blowing spark in tinder

Figures 26, 27, and 28. ***Ishi working fire drill.***
(Courtesy of Lowie Museum of Anthropology, University of California at Berkeley.)

Figure 29. *Binding of salmon spear completed.*
(Courtesy of Lowie Museum of Anthropology, University of California at Berkeley.)

Figure 30. ***Cutting juniper wood for a bow with an adz.***
(Courtesy of Lowie Museum of Anthropology, University of California at Berkeley.)

Figure 31. *Shooting from kneeling position, the preferred shooting stance of Yahi hunters*
(Courtesy of Lowie Museum of Anthropology, University of California at Berkeley.)

Figure 32. *Black tail deer*
(Courtesy of Bob Price)

Figure 33. *Retrieving an arrow*
(Courtesy of Lowie Museum of Anthropology,
University of California at Berkeley.)

Figure 34. *Skinning a deer.*
(Courtesy of Lowie Museum of Anthropology,
University of California at Berkeley.)

Sources

[1] A.L. Kroeber, "Ishi the Last Aborigine," *The World's Work* (July, 1912).

[2] Tape by Adolf F. Kessler describing "Ishi's Capture," given to me in 1973 by Robert Hewitt, second cousin to Adolf Kessler. Three facts of contention with Kroeber's book that Mr. Kessler said on tape were: (1) Ishi's name was given Ishi by Sheriff Webber; (2) that the apron Ishi was wearing was not given Ishi by a butcher. It was not a butcher's apron, but that of a Mexican miner. Ishi possibly stole the apron from Apperson's supply cabin or somewhere; (3) Ishi was not afraid of the train when he had to board it in Oroville. He didn't seem excited or scared when boarding. He was carrying his shoes in his hands.

[3] Eva Marie Apperson, *We Knew Ishi* (Red Bluff, California: Walker Lithograph Company, 1971), p. 77.

[4] *Ibid.*

[5] Theodora Kroeber, *Ishi in Two Worlds* (Berkeley: University of California Press, 1961), pp. 6-7.

[6] Edward Sapir and Leslie Spier, *Anthropological Records 3:3 Notes on the Culture of the Yana* (Berkeley: UC Press, 1943), p. 72.

[7] T.T. Waterman, in *Southern Workman,* XLVI (1917), 528-537.

[8] Theodora Kroeber, *op. cit*, pp. 84-85.

[9] A.L. Kroeber, *op. cit.*, p. 11.

[10] T.T. Waterman, "The Yana Indians: Discovery of the Yahi Village in 1908," *California University Publication in American Archaeology and Ethnology* XIII (1917-1923), p. 60.

[11] *Ibid.*

[12] Tape by Adolf F. Kessler *op. cit.*

[13] Theodora Kroeber, *op. cit.*, p. 161.

[14] *Ibid*, pp. 173-174.

[15] *Ibid*, pp. 193, 194-195.

[16] *Ibid*, p. 218. This source states the "homeward train ride" as the day of June 1, 1914.

[17] *Ibid*, p. 217.

[18] J.C. Hunt, "When Lassen Blew Its Stack," *American Forest* (June 1972) 78, pp. 28-31.

[19] Apperson, *op. cit.*, p. 6.

[20] Apperson, *op. cit.*, pp. 8-9, 25.

[21] Theodora Kroeber, *op. cit.*, pp. 237-238.

[22] Story and permission courtesy of Herb Puffer of Pacific Western Traders, Folsom, California.

Figure 35.
Ishi and Companion at Iamin Mool by Concow Maidu artist Frank Day.
(Reprinted courtesy of Herb Puffer, Pacific Western Traders, Folsom, CA).

Unusual Ishi Encounter as Told by Frank Day

Here is a mysterious episode in the life of Ishi that is little known, as related by Concow Maidu artist Frank Day who lived from 1902 to 1976.

One bright, warm morning in late July 1911, Frank Day (then nine years old) and his father Twoboe were strolling along an old wagon road not far from where the forks of Feather River come together at a place called *Iamin Mool* by the Concow Maidu people. They had just visited friends nearby where they had passed the night and were headed home — when they suddenly came upon the strange scene depicted in this painting (see Figure 36). Sensing their intrusion on a private and urgent situation involving strangers, but understandably intrigued by the sight, Frank and Twoboe lingered behind some roadside brush to observe.

The person kneeling at the left was later identified as Ishi, who was captured a few days later near Oroville. Although no other record has come to light indicating that Ishi had left his homeland in Mill Creek Canyon with a fellow tribesman, such appeared to be the case to Frank and his father. The man reclining beneath the oak was garbed similar to Ishi and wore his hair in identical fashion. It was evident to the observers that he suffered from a gunshot wound in his stomach and that Ishi was treating the wound by what seemed to be an ingeniously contrived heat application.

At the left, a slab of mica (a mineral common in that area), caught around the center of some kind of flexible material and lashed to a stake in the ground, has been placed so as to catch the rays of the hot summer sun and cast them onto a vessel that has been filled with water or some herbal mixture. From a gnarled limb of the overhanging oak, a rope fashioned from some native fibre has been suspended. Pestle-shaped stones are secured at either end of the rope. The patient holds one stone with his right hand and is applying it against his wound, while Ishi holds the rope in his left hand and the opposite stone rests against his left knee. About to place the stone into the bowl, Ishi looks up, startled, into the eyes of Twoboe, who with Frank stands just a few feet away partially concealed. No words were exchanged and the onlookers quietly withdrew, sensing that their further intrusion was not invited.

A second encounter with Ishi occurred at Oroville Jail, where he was held in custody for a time after capture. In an effort to communicate with the "wild man," the sheriff called upon Twoboe to try talking with Ishi in the Concow language, and so Frank and his father visited the bewildered captive. There was an instant recognition of each other from the trail incident, but Twoboe understood no Yahi and so no verbal communication could be established. The fate of the wounded companion, his identity and clarification of the witnessed procedure, remain mysteries. Over sixty years later, Frank's keen perception for detail, a trait ingrained by Twoboe's training, enabled him to record this mystifying, historic cameo.[22]

Annual Ishi Contest Is Held At California State Indian Museum

Every year the California State Indian Museum sponsors an essay, poetry, and drawing contest on the subject of Ishi. Entries are solicited from children in the fourth, fifth, and sixth grades and the winning selections are displayed in the museum for a year. The staff of the museum has decided to interpret the story of Ishi through the eyes of school children who have learned about Ishi by visiting the museum, reading books, and watching educational films. Except for the identification of the photographs and artifacts, Ishi is seen here from their point of view...

Figure 36. ***Ishi Day.***

Reactions By 4th, 5th, and 6th Graders

In April, 1911, Ishi came into the white man's world. In this New World, he discovered that there were good and bad white men, just like there were good and bad Indians...

...After five years of living in San Francisco, Ishi made one trip back to the Yahi World with Dr. Kroeber and three friends. The men lived as Ishi lived — hunting with bow and arrows, fishing, taking sweat baths, gathering berries over a month. On this trip, the white men gained a better understanding and a lasting appreciation for the Indian way.

Karen Pangilinan
4th Grade, Starr King School

Ishi was a special man,
He was generous and wise.
He liked to hunt,
  and he liked to play.
He was not just an American,
He was an American Indian.
He brought to our city
  the language of his people.

Abraham
6th Grade

An Indian called Ishi,
Is from a tribe called Yahi.
Most of the relatives were shot,
Ishi and just a few were not.
Living in a canyon all alone,
He had no place for his own.
He died alone and very old,
Because he caught a white-man's cold.

Christy Jones
4th Grade, Springview School

Nobody could ever find them when they were walking because they would jump from rock to rock or crawl through some brush where not even a deer could fit through.

Justine Burge
5th Grade, Marple School

I think Ishi was very important. And he was a great man. He taught me that the Yahi people were very skilled. The Yahi had more right on this land than we do. Ishi's tribe was killed off and that was not fair at all...

...I understand what a great loss Ishi's death was. My great-grandfather was a California Indian. So I know how much he meant to us.

Stephan Van Zant
4th Grade, Skycrest School

Ishi thought that the white man's civilization was clever, but not very wise.

Sara Salazar
Shoshoni/Paiute
5th Grade, Maple

A man stumbling into a place of many valleys and mountains of wood and concrete with horses of steel that walk on wheels.

Clayton Williamsen
6th Grade, Howe Avenue School

Ishi lived in the wilderness
all alone and by himself,
with no books up on a shelf.
He was the last of his tribe.
The very last to survive.
Although he brought
us so much history,
much about his life
remains still a mystery.

Tami Green
6th Garde, St. Francis School

Examination

(25 points)

1. Ishi means ________________________________ in Yana.

2-3. Ishi "came in" to ________________________________ on August 29, ______.
(town) (year)

4. Ishi was discovered on his haunches:
   a. in front of the county jail
   b. in the cave by Mill Creek
   c. in a slaughterhouse in a V-shaped corral
   d. in the woods by the Graham's cabin

5. One day, Ishi made up his mind to "come in." He expected:
   a. that he would be taken captive and turned over to the authorities
   b. to be killed, but that no longer mattered
   c. to be sent to a *rancheria* near Chico with other Indians
   d. to see some of his tribal friends who had lived with him

6. The person who first discovered Ishi was:
   a. Adolf Kessler, who used a gambrel
   b. Floyd Phillip Heffner, a 10 year old
   c. Mr. Apperson, who owned land on Deer Creek
   d. T. T. Waterman, the anthropologist

7. Ishi had shorn his hair because:
   a. it was too long
   b. he was in mourning
   c. so people wouldn't recognize him
   d. it was a custom when meeting new people

8. What did Ishi have in his ears? (short essay)

   ____

9. What was inserted in Ishi's nasal septum? (Hint: At puberty this object was awarded and to be worn at death to help guarantee passage to the other world.)

   ____

10. Ishi's language tribe was ____________________ while his tribelet was Yahi.

11. T.T. Waterman got Ishi to respond when he said:
    a. *Kum* which means house dwelling place
    b. *Siwini* which means yellow pine
    c. *Ceu* which means water
    d. *Noto* which means "east-water."

12. From 1911 to 1916 Ishi lived in:
    a. Berkeley
    b. Oakland
    c. Sacramento
    d. San Francisco

13. True or False: It was Yahi Indian propriety to say one's real name out land whenever asked.

14. *Wa gan u p'a* means:

a. Mount Shasta | b. Mount Rose
c. Mount Lassen | d. Mount Diablo

15. True or False: *Ha t'an en* was a "fabulous malignant water grizzly" that lived in the waters along the valley's Sacramento River who would pull fishermen down to devour them.

16. The Peter Lassen trail went:

a. from Salt Lake City to Sacramento
b. across the crest between Mill Creek and Deer Creek
c. Canada via the Oregon trail
d. Red Bluff and then to Redding

17. What happened at Kingsley Cave in 1865? (short essay)

____

18. For forty years, ______________ (number) survivors took refuge in the utterly wild canyon

19. On November 9, 1908, two men with the Oro Water Light and Power Company suddenly:

a. saved thirty Indians who were drowning
b. saw a naked Indian standing on a rock armed with a long spear
c. saw three rattlesnakes bite a lone Indian named Ishi
d. realized that their flume would collapse on top of an Indian village site

20. Bear's Hiding Place (*Wowunupo'mu*) was discovered on the ______________ (compass orientation) side of ______________ (name) creek.

21. Found in camp under some blankets (in 1908) was:

a. a partially paralyzed old woman | b. bows, arrows and fire sticks
c. army ammunition. | a sack of poisoned wheat

22. Professor Kroeber gave Ishi a job as: ______________

23. Next to glue, Ishi rated ______________ (item) civilization's most important invention.

24. What happened on May 30, 1914, just as Ishi was leaving his homeland for good?

____

25. On March 25, 1916, the last "wild" Indian of North America died of:

a. tuberculosis | b. Small pox
c. malaria | d. cholera

Answers

1. Man 2.-3. Oroville, 1911 4. c 5. b 6. b 7. b 8. buckskin string 9. a small, wooden nose plug 10. Yana 11. b 12. d 13. false 14. c 15. true 16. b 17. massacre 18. five 19. b 20. south, Deer 21. a 22. assistant janitor of the museum 23. matches 24. sacred Mt. Lassen erupted 25. a

Other Books By Richard Burrill

River of Sorrows

In this inspiring historical novel, Richard Burrill combines careful scholarship and skillful writing to provide a realistic "window" into the Maidu-Nisenan Indian cultures and their transition from Stone Age culture to the modern Iron Age. Through the eyes of Tokiwa, a Nisenan medicine doctor, we witness the end of a peaceful and prosperous era and experience the tragedy of his people's destruction. *River of Sorrows* depicts the beauty and intimacy of tribal tradition and oration, as well as reveas the struggles and conflicts among themselves and with the encroaching and deceptive white man.

River of Sorrows uplifts the ageless wisdom of old Native American ways, and is an original and unique contribution to California history.

$8.95

ISBN 0-87961-187-1

The Human Almanac

Many topics appear in *The Human Almanac*. This is an excellent reference book for those of us who usually do not have enough time to step outside our own fields and explore some of the most discussed, yet unanswered, topics of our times. *The Human Almanac* asks: What is the substance of man? Who are we as a species? Where do we come from? What are alternative ways of looking at our popular culture, free from the prejudices of our past and present?

A great gift for friend or student, as it belongs in every American home and public library. An ideal book for those who want to improve their cultural literacy.

The Human Almanac blows the mind because it is about us!

$10.95

ISBN 0-943238-00-5

Protectors of the Land

For thousands of yearsthey lived in harmony with the Earth. They came to possess a deeply rooted conservation ethic because their leaders knew about the nature of spiritual power. Descendants still live today and proudly carry on their unique cultural heritage.

This book teaches how to be a keen observer, keeping the children at the center of their learning encounters.

$19.95

Ordering Information

Please Print, Copy, and Send

Name ______________________________

Address ______________________ Apt. No. ________

City ______________________ State ___ Zip ________

Phone (   ) ______________________

Quantity	Titles	Price	Subtotals
_____	Ishi	$9.50	__________
_____	The Human Almanac	$10.95	__________
_____	River of Sorrows	$8.95	__________
_____	Protectors of the Land	$19.95	__________
_____	Map: California Indians	$7.95	__________
_____	Map: Eagle's Eye Over Northern California	$7.95	__________
	Total List Price of Items Ordered		__________
	Subtract _____% Professional Discount		__________
	Discounted TOTAL		__________
	California Residents Add Local Sales Tax		__________
	Shipping & Handling		__________
	TOTAL PAYMENT ENCLOSED		__________

Shipping and handling charges of $2.00 added to each $10 purchase; $7.50 over $100.

Bookstore wholesale price:

1-0	20%
10-24	40%
25-49	42%
50+	45%

Applies to books shipped to one location only. 40% discount if prepaid, including postage

Library Discount	10%
School Discount	20%

Method of Payment

❑ Check or money order enclosed
Payable to The Anthro Company

❑ Visa ❑ Mastercard

❑ American Express

Card # ______________________

Expiration Date ______________________

Signature ______________________________

Would you like a copy of the current catalog? ________

Order from:

THE ANTHRO COMPANY

P.O. Box 661765 Sacramento, CA 95866-1765 (916) 971-1675

30-day money back guarantee.